WINNING

Seattle Real Estate

2nd Edition

by

Dan Sanchez

Managing Broker

Coldwell Banker Danforth

Instructor

Washington State Housing Finance
Commission

Copyright

Table of Contents

Highlights

You will never win against someone who requires something that you don't really care about.

In my opinion, only 20% of brokers have the knowledge attributed to all brokers. The vast majority of brokers are better at getting your business than they are at actually representing you.

Buyers don't normally have to pay for their broker.

The buyer's broker works for the buyer, and the listing agent works for the seller. The State of Washington is very clear about this.

If you want the same results as someone else, then you have to do what they did.

You can actually buy a house contingent on the sale of your existing house- even in this hot market.

Introduction

My average buyer buys the first house they make an offer on. I know it is hard to believe since the average buyer in Seattle makes an offer on 5 or more houses before they win. My clients and loan officers know my track record. I got tired of them telling me to write a book...So I finally did it!

This book is for first timers and experience home owners. Some of the facts and names were changed to protect the innocent (and not so innocent).

Here is a joke I tell all my new clients: A homeowner has a leaky pipe in his basement. Over the course of a year, he tries to fix it, but every time he does, he makes it worse.

Finally, he calls an expert—a plumber. The plumber looks at the pipe, looks in his bag and then pulls out a wrench. The plumber taps the pipe with the wrench, and the leak stops.

The homeowner can't believe his eyes but is angry when presented with a $200 invoice. He demands to know how the price is broken down.

The plumber says: "$1 for pulling the wrench out of my bag and $199 for knowing where to tap the pipe with my wrench!"

I tell all my clients that joke at the beginning of our relationship. It usually get's a laugh; however, it is amazing how many times I have to refer back to that joke after I have solved a problem or saved a ton of money for someone!

1

Today's Market Environment

My average buyer buys the first house they write an offer on. I am going to show you how you can too.

If you see any terms that you don't understand then you may find the definitions in the section called Common Questions.

It used to be that listings would come online any day of the week. This changed when the market got hot. These days sellers expect multiple offers on their property and they have found that setting up a bid -review date is a good way to do it. They do this by stating that they will review offers only on a particular date. This is usually about 5-7 days after the listing date. For some reason listing brokers don't include this information in their public marketing! The only wau you would know that there is a bid review date is by asking a real estate agent.

Most new listings come online on Wednesday or Thursday with a bid review date of the following Tuesday or Wednesday. They structure it this way so that they can do some open houses that end within a few days of when offers are due.

Three times as many listings go live on Wed and Thurs than on Monday and Tues.

The seller can choose to accept an offer before the bid review date. This would almost always be an all cash offer with no contingencies and a quick close for well above the listed price.

In almost every case -the seller will not even look at any offers that have an inspection contingency or where the offered price is below the list price. This is because the inspection contingency is a "walk away" clause -meaning that the buyer can walk away for no reason at all during the inspection period. In a normal market environment the buyer would be able to inspect the property after the contract has been agreed to.

An offer review date puts the buyers in the position of having to inspect the property before they even write an offer (if they want a competitive offer) This can easily cost $600! It can get expensive and emotionally exhausting if you lose out on a few of these bid wars. Some buyers even give up by the time summer rolls around because they are tired. Its called buyer fatigue and it is a real thing.

Since the seller is expecting multiple offers on the review date, they are not very interested in looking at offers before that date unless it is truly too good to pass up. Even if the property is clearly over priced, the seller will usually not consider a reasonable offer until the bid review date comes and goes. A bid review date is a clear statement that the seller expects more than the list price. Sometimes the seller gets a real education when no one shows up with an offer on that date.

Sometimes no one shows up on the bid review date though. The median market time in Seattle is around 7 days. As you probably know, median means half sell before 7 days and half sell after 7 days. Sellers seem to forget this and rather believe that all houses sell in less than 7 days. Believe it or not, if a house is on the market for more than 7 days then there is a 50% chance it will still be for sale after a month!

Buyers and sellers assume that the property will sell for at least 10% more than the list price in a multiple bid situation. Buyers also know that the seller expects to see offers with no inspection contingency.

If the property isn't marketed right or if it is priced a little too high then it is possible that the bid review date will arrive and there will be no offers. If a buyer thinks they don't have much chance at winning then they might decide not to spend the $600 to write the offer! In other words the property may be worth $650,000 but if buyers don't think its worth $700,000 then they may not be willing to risk paying for an inspection. They may think that they don't have much chance of winning because they are unwilling to pay more than the list price. I= A bid review date with no offers happens more often than people think. It is a terrible feeling to be the seller or listing broker when this happens.

If the bid review date passes then buyers will think something is wrong with the property even if there isn't. It could be worth the list price but no one made an offer because they didn't want to more than the list price...especially if they are expected to pay for an inspection before they even make the offer. The seller will have a hard time selling the property now though because buyers will now assume that something is wrong with the property!

This actually happened on one of my own listings. We priced it a little too high and no one made an offer on the bid review date. About 3 weeks later a couple came through the open house who had looked at it on the first weekend but they didn't make an offer because they couldn't pay above the listed price. They assumed it would sell on the bid date for more than list price. They never bothered to check that it was still for sale afterward. They later happened to be driving by when I was holding my 3rd open house and discovered it was still available. They bought the property for $5,000 less than the price.

So how do you compete in this hot market? First it is important to have a broker who can write a 'clean' offer with no mistakes. Don't give the seller a stupid reason to make a counter offer because they might decide to add in some changes that they didn't really care about the first time. Only about 20% of brokers have the knowledge that the public attributes to all of them. Picking a broker that won't mess up the offer is critical. 80% of real estate agents are better at getting your business than they are at doing their job.

You will never win a bid against someone who needs something that you don't care about. For example; I always ask new buyers if they need three bedrooms on the same floor. If they say "no" then I tell them not to even bother looking at houses like that. This is because many buyers that are starting a family require three bedrooms on the same floor...and they will out bid you every time.

You have your best chances of winning by going after houses that have a unique feature that most people find annoying, but which you don't mind. Maybe you prefer to have a master bedroom in the basement. You would have a good shot at this house because it is a configuration that many people don't care about. One of the most valuable skills I bring to the table is: knowing which houses you have the best chance of winning.

If you are competing with multiple offers then you will likely have an Escalation Clause. One of the most frustrating things about this market is the way Escalation Clauses work. An Escalation Clause is a form that simply says that you will pay X amount more than the next buyer up to Y price. Sounds simple, right? You can find more information in the Common Questions section.

Let's say you are trying to buy a house priced at $500,000 and you are willing to pay as much as $550,000 – then you might be willing to pay $5,000 more than the next highest offer up to $550,000. The next question your broker will ask is, "Will you be sad if someone else paid $5,000 more than that?" ($555,000) Usually, the answer is yes. So you increase your limit to $560,000. Then the next question is, "Would you be sad if someone else paid only $565,000?" This goes on and on until the buyer finds a number that they are hoping they won't have to pay -a pain threshold -which they usually wind up having to pay. But wait, it gets better (actually, it gets worse).

If you know that you will be going up against multiple offers, then you have to focus on all the aspects of the contract, not just the price. This means waiving as many contingencies as you feel comfortable with. (A contingency is a predetermined way that the buyer can back out of the deal and get their earnest money returned to them. Waiving a contingency means giving up that right.)

The most common contingencies are the Inspection Contingency and the Finance Contingency. In a normal market environment, the buyer would be able to negotiate a period of time (usually a few days) in which they can inspect the property. During this period the buyer can back out of the transaction and have their earnest money returned - even without a reason! You can see why sellers may not like this! In a multiple offer situation, your offer will likely be thrown away if it has an Inspection Contingency.

So how do you know the property isn't a lemon? You inspect it BEFORE you write the offer. This is called a pre-inspection. It can cost around $600 and takes about 3 hours. That is $600 for each house that you write an offer on. Can you see how painful this can get if you lose a few bids?

Making your offer seem as close to a cash offer as possible is very important. The benefits of a cash offer to the seller is that they typically do not have an appraisal involved and they close very quickly   It takes a few weeks for a lender to be certain about you, your ability to borrow, and the quality of the property. Cash offers can typically close in about 10 days.

If you are obtaining financing, then you would most likely want a Finance Contingency. This allows you to back out of the transaction and have your earnest money returned if you are unable to obtain your financing during a certain period of time. Part of the Finance Contingency is the appraisal. The way the standard agreement is written, you don't have to pay more than the appraised price. In this market it is common for prices to be higher than the appraisal.   Buyers who have a high level of confidence in their financing might not include a finance contingency. They simply risk losing their earnest money if they aren't able to get financing.

Many sellers are asking the buyer to waive all or part of the appraisal before they even accept your offer. For example, if the seller thinks the property will appraise for $600,000 but your offer is $650,000 then they might ask you to cover the difference. This means that you would have to pay an additional $50,000 on top of your downpayment.

If you have an 80% loan to value loan then the lender is only going to lend 80% of the amount of the appraisal. So your down payment would be 20% of $600,000 PLUS $50,000 or $170,000 ($120,000+$50,000), instead of 20% of $650,000 which would be $130,000. Make sure to do your math before you offer to waive part of the appraisal.

Shortening the closing time is also critical. One way to do this is to get Pre-Underwritten for your loan. Some lenders don't like the term Pre-Underwritten and may have a different name for the process.

Getting pre underwritten is different than getting pre-qualified. Many lenders will give you a pre-qualification letter based on the income and expenses that you tell them. Sometimes you can just fill out an online form which will generate a prequalification letter for you.

In the past you would apply for the loan after you have a mutually agreed up purchase and sale agreement, at which time you would be asked to provide pay stubs, tax returns, credit card bills etc. This process can take a couple of weeks. Getting pre- underwritten means that you provide those documents before you even find a house to make an offer on. This allows your lender to get you the money 2 weeks faster once you have a property under contract.

Your lender might normally require 35 days to fund your purchase but if you have been pre-underwritten then they might be able to do it in less than 20 days. This is a big deal to sellers.

The buyer also has 3 days to back out upon receiving the Form 17. This is a huge list of disclosures about the property that the seller is required to fill out. A smart listing broker will make sure that the prospective buyers have this before the offer review date. A competitive buyer will read it, acknowledge receipt and waive the 3 day period.

If the property is a condominium, then there will be a list of disclosures made by the condominium association called a Resale Certificate. Larger condominium projects are also required to include a Reserve Study which is a written inspection of the property that includes the useful life of the different building components, the cost of replacement, and whether or not the association is collecting enough dues to pay for replacements. Sometimes this can take a few weeks for the association to put together. It can also be hundreds of pages long. Surprisingly many listing brokers do not have this available by the time that offers are due. If it is available then a competitive buyer will read it, acknowledge receipt and waive the review period.

If you are not in a hurry to buy a home you might consider only writing offers on properties that have been on the market for more than 10 days.

Sometimes a house doesn't sell on the offer review date. This can happen if the price is too high, or if it is too close to the actual value. Buyers usually assume that a property will sell for at least 5-10% more than the list price. The house might be worth the list price—but not 10% more than the list price...so it gets no offers on the offer review date. Listing brokers know that it is very difficult to get the listing price after the offer review date has passed. You can use this to your advantage by writing an offer the day after the offers are due. You might even get an inspection contingency and a full financing contingency.

Here is an example: Let's say a seller is trying to sell a house that should be worth $25,000 more than comparable houses. Let's say these other houses were listed around $850,000 and sold for $900,000 -if the house in question is listed for $925,000 then buyers will assume the seller wants 10% more at least (over $1million) , which is way higher than the comps. In this situation it is very possible that no buyers will even make an offer. The seller will now have a very hard time getting the list price and might even need to reduce it to $875,000. Instead, if it were listed for $875,000 then it might get escalated to $925,000.

Prices tend to increase in January when inventory is at its lowest. This is because it takes one or two months to get a house ready for market and people don't want to work on their house during the holidays so they wait until mid January to start. If you have a choice it is better to buy in fall rather than after the new year...or after June.

A buyer, on the other hand, only has to get their checkbook out to be ready. In January, there are lots of buyers and very little inventory. In June there are sellers and very little buyers. June can also be a good time to buy.

June (after school is out) is a good time to be a buyer. Buyers who are still looking for a house at this time frequently give up or are preoccupied with other summer activities. Interest in new listings drops dramatically around this time which gives buyers a great opportunity.

2

Why you can't put a house in a Shopping Cart

There has been a recent wave of companies tricking new home buyers into thinking that you should be able to buy a house the same way that you buy earbuds on Amazon...by putting it in a shopping cart. Well a set of earbuds doesn't come with a contract with dozens of different conditions and circumstances in which you could lose thousands of dollars because you as the buyer failed to do something.

There may be some things I am not smart about but I am definitely not stupid enough to enter into a 22 page contract to buy something for hundreds of thousands of dollars that commits me to THIRTY YEARS of monthly payments of $4,000 a month without having an expert in that field help me!

There is a mortgage company on TV that makes it seem like they have some amazing new technology where in fact almost every single lender I know offers the same type of service. They make it seem as if you will never touch a piece of paper. The truth is that they will later ask you to dig up credit card bills and old tax returns after you fill out an online form. You may have these in digital format which is great...guess what?...Every lender I know will also accept digital copies of these documents.

Almost all lenders can also generate a prequalification letter from a simple online form. (which by the way is almost worthless in a hot market) Pre-Underwriting is better and this will take a matter of days no matter who your lender is.

Sooner or later though you will have to sign 120 pages of documents in the physical presence of a notary whether it is an online lender or not. Why? Because a 30 year mortgage is a 30 year contract with a future value of over a million dollars (including interest)! No mortgage company on the planet will let you docusign a Deed of Trust.

You may be used to signing up for websites without reading the terms of service...but if you sign a contract without reading it then you may wind up losing all of your life savings in the blink of an eye. You can't replace a trusted expert that has experience with the document that you are signing. Can you fix a car just because you watch Jay Leno's garage? You can't be a successful home investor just because you have watched HG Channel "reality" shows.

The Multiple Listing Service provides standard contracts that its members are required to use when selling a house that is listed on the MLS. It has silly details in it in it...like when does a day end? No the day does not end at midnight... it ends at 9pm in Washington State. If you have a 1 day inspection and it is Friday then you have until Saturday at 9pm right? Wrong- You have until Monday at 9pm. What if you have a 5 day inspection and it is Friday? You have until the following Friday. Now check this out....What if you have a 7 day inspection and it is Friday? - You have until the following Friday. This is because any period of time of 5 days or less is counted in Business days, otherwise counted in Calendar days.

Did you know that sellers in WA state have to provide a list of disclosures to the buyer? or that the buyer has 3 days to back out of the deal after they get it? There would be no way for you to know that. There is not any language in the Purchase and Sale Agreement that says anything about this. It just happens to be Washington State law.

I could write 10 more pages about things in the purchase and sale agreement (and things that aren't) that are not obvious. I have many stories of people getting burned because they thought they were saving money by not hiring a realtor. Also guess what? -If you are the buyer then you don't even have to pay upfront for your realtor? The seller has probably already agreed to allow the seller broker and the buyer broker to be paid from closing proceeds. The seller doesn't pay less if only one broker is involved. (and no you don't benefit from going direct to the listing broker unless you want your advice to come from someone who has a State mandated responsibility to look after the seller's interest instead of yours)

Buying a house is a complicated process that varies by State. Anyone who makes it seem like you can just click a couple of boxes to buy a house is pulling your leg. Of course by the time you find this out...it is too late. You are already committed and now you have to go through the same process as everyone else. This is what they are counting on.

3

Getting Started

Step 1: Choose an Experienced Buyer's Agent

I think that only about 20% of all real estate agents have the level of knowledge attributed to all real estate agents. In other words, the level of knowledge that the public believes that real estate agents have is only possessed by around 1/5th of all real estate agents. In other words 80% of brokers are better at getting business than they are at actually doing their jobs. So, a great broker is really hard to find and really bad ones practically fall in your lap!

An experienced and savvy buyer's agent can save you thousands of dollars throughout the property purchase process and will offer you valuable insights on a wide range of topics throughout your search for a home. A bad broker can really cause problems. Think about that for a minute. How bad can it be? I had a situation in which a lender required a government FHA form to be signed by the seller and buyer a few days before closing. The listing broker couldn't wrap his head around the language and for some reason thought that his seller was going to be harmed by signing it. The lender and the government required this to be signed. The listing broker completely disappeared for 3 days. We couldn't get a hold of him until the evening of the day that we were supposed to close (and that was only because I finally called his manager). He almost torpedoed his own transaction which would have created a possible financial liability for his seller....just because he never did an FHA financed transaction before, didn't understand the language, and didn't ask for help.

A knowledgeable buyer's agent can help guide you on how much you should pay for a particular home, suggest the best mortgage lenders and inspectors to work with and offer you the valuable advice you can only get from a real estate professional with extensive experience in the local market. Additionally, there are a few buyer's agents that offer special incentives such as buyer cash back programs and down payment assistance you never have to repay!

If you only follow one of the steps we have included in this list, it should be this one: partnering with a great real estate agent is many times the single most important factor in searching for a new home and successfully completing a purchase.

Step 2: Discuss Your Needs with Your Buyer's Agent

Once you select an agent to work with, it is important to have a detailed initial meeting to discuss all the details of your situation with your agent. Keep in mind a buyer's agent should represent you and you alone. You do not want to work with a transaction agent who is working for both the buyer and the seller. A transaction agent has no fiduciary responsibility to either party and as such can disclose everything to the seller and vice versa. A buyer's agent's purpose is to negotiate for you alone, always having your best interest in mind, and to do everything they can to put you in the best possible negotiating position. They will review all your disclosures and laws so you have an understanding of the legal requirements of the home buying process. Therefore, it's important to openly discuss all the important aspects of your new home search with your agent, including any financial concerns, family issues or any items that you absolutely cannot do without.

The better they understand your overall personal circumstances, the more effective they can be at helping you achieve all your objectives and requirements. Obviously, the topics discussed during your initial meeting will vary quite a bit from person to person, depending on your main concerns. However, the key areas below are typically the minimum amount of topics that should be covered during the meeting. Remember: the broker you choose to work with will most likely be paid by the listing broker.

Financial Situation and Challenges
If you have any special requirements, limitations, or credit issues, now is the time to discuss them with your agent. If you are upfront and honest about it, then they can help you find viable solutions to any existing issues. If you choose to hold back information, then they may not find out until it is too late for them to offer you help and/or save the deal. Remember, your buyer's agent is on your side and there to help you.

Step 3: Finding a Lender
Establish Initial Price Range/Budget
You should always establish a budget in terms of monthly payment and total price before you begin shopping for a home.

Pre-Approval and completing the Mortgage Approval Process
Get some recommendations for which lenders might offer you the best options. Obtaining a mortgage pre-approval or pre-qualification is a crucial step in the home buying process.

Having a lender review your financial situation and give you a formal pre-approval letter will let sellers know you are not only willing to purchase their home but also able to make a purchase. In fact, some sellers will not even consider an offer unless you have gone through the lender pre- qualification process. It's important to take care of this step very early on in the process and to keep your buyer's agent informed of any communication or extra requirements of the lender.

4

About Mortgages

What is a Mortgage?

A mortgage is a loan secured by your home. They are typically 30 years in duration but people frequently opt for a 15 year plan. Your first payments are only going towards the interest, no loan amount is being paid off. This gradually changes over time until most of your payment is paying off the loan amount.

What is PMI (Private Mortgage Insurance)

This is an insurance policy that a lender might require you to purchase depending on the type of loan that you are applying for and depending on your downpayment. It insures them against a loss in the event that they foreclose on your house and sell it for less than the loan amount. PMI can definitely add hundreds of dollars a month to your loan amount and could actually cause you to qualify for a lower loan amount. There is a tradeoff between low downpayment because PMI can make your actual monthly payments go up more than you might think.

Fixed Rate Mortgage vs Adjustable Rate Mortgage

A fixed rate mortgage means that your interest rate would stay the same during the entire 30 year term of the loan.

An Adjustable Rate Mortgage (ARM) is one in which your rate will be adjusted (up or down) depending on prevailing interest rates at the time. There is a limit as to how much the adjustment can be. Also they only adjust every few years. It just depends on the exact terms of the ARM that you apply for. Talk to a mortgage broker about the different programs.

Jumbo Loans (also called Non-Conforming)

A Jumbo Loan is NOT backed by the government because it is larger than the government limits.. This is why they are called Non-Conforming Loans. Examples of government backed loans are FNMA (Fannie Mae), FDMC (Freddie Mac), FHA, and VA. The government will back loans up to $667,000 in King, Snohomish, and Pierce Counties (as of June 2018) Jumbo Loans are NOT government back and are larger than $667,000 in these areas are called Jumbo Loans.

Conforming Loans (FNMA, FDMC, FHA, VA)

Downpayment Assistance from Washington State are compatible with these loans (even the low downpayment options) as long as guidelines are met. Some lenders are offering 1% down when the two programs are put together.

FNMA (Fannie Mae) & FDMC (Freddie Mac)

These are Conforming Loans. FNMA and FDMC both buy loans from banks as long as the banks make sure that the borrower meets strict requirements. This makes it easier for banks to loan money because they know they have a ready buyer for the loan.

FHA and VA

FHA and VA (The Veterans Administration) are also called Conforming Loans. They both insure banks against losses. This makes it easier for banks to lend money because their losses are insured as long as the buyer meets the strict requirements.

Lown down payment plans from FHA and VA

Here is information about FNMA, FDMC, FHA, and VA loans directly from their websites. Call your friendly neighborhood mortgage broker or banker for more information. If you don't know one, call me and I will give you some names of people that can help you.

FHA Low Down Payment Details

The Federal Housing Administration (FHA) mortgage insurance program is managed by the Department of Housing and Urban Development (HUD), which is a department of the federal government. FHA loans are available to all types of borrowers, not just first-time buyers. The government insures the lender against losses that might result from borrower default. Advantage: This program allows you to make a down payment as low as 3.5% of the purchase price. Disadvantage: You'll have to pay for mortgage insurance, which will increase the size of your monthly payments.

First-time homebuyers who can't afford a large down payment but would otherwise qualify for a home loan may be eligible for a 3% down payment mortgage. If you're good at managing your credit and meet certain requirements, this could be the option for you.

A mortgage lender can provide the specifics, assess your financial situation, and determine eligibility. But before you contact a lender, consider these initial requirements:

At least one person on the loan must be a first-time homebuyer. (In this case, "first-time homebuyer" means that you haven't owned any residential property in the past three years. Or, if you're buying the home with someone else, at least one of you hasn't owned a home in the past three years.)
The home being financed must be a one-unit property (including townhomes, condos, co-ops, and PUDs) and not a manufactured home.

You plan to occupy the home as your primary residence; and
The mortgage must have a fixed rate (adjustable rate mortgages [ARMs] are not eligible for the 3% down payment mortgage).

VA Low Down Payment Details
Most VA Home Loans are handled entirely by private lenders and VA rarely gets involved in the loan approval process. VA "stands behind" the loan by guaranteeing a portion of it. If something goes wrong and you can't make the payments anymore, the lending institution can come to us to cover any losses they might incur. The VA loan guaranty is the "insurance" that we provide the lender.

VA Home Loan Advantages
The guarantee VA provides to lenders allows them to provide you with more favorable terms, including:

No down payment as long as the sales price doesn't exceed the appraised value.

No private mortgage insurance premium requirement.

VA rules limit the amount you can be charged for closing costs.

Closing costs may be paid by the seller.

The lender can't charge you a penalty fee if you pay the loan off early.

VA may be able to provide you some assistance if you run into difficulty making payments.

You should also know that:

You don't have to be a first-time homebuyer.
You can reuse the benefit.
VA-backed loans are assumable,

5

I want to make an offer

What happens after you find a house you want to buy? You fill out the Purchase and Sale Agreement with your broker. First you fill out these forms.

The Purchase and Sale Agreement is not a single document It is a collection of forms that might total around 22 pages more or less. All brokers who are part of the Multiple Listing Service use the same forms that are provided by the MLS.

Form 21 is five pages and is the main part. The first page has the details of your offer including a list of what other forms are part of the agreement. The last four pages of this agreement consists of pre-printed fine print that most people don't read but YOU SHOULD READ. It says that the end of the day is 9pm. Any time frame of 5 days or less is business days not calendar days. Things like that. Important details are in there.

Form 22A is the Finance Addendum. This will show how much down payment you have, what type of loan you are getting, what happens if the appraisal is low. If you change these details after mutual acceptance...and you don't get the loan...you might lose your earnest money.

Form 22D is Optional Clauses. It is a 2 page form of miscellaneous clauses. Things like; does the seller have to clean the house before closing; who owns the stuff the seller leaves behind, etc. (I usually tell my buyers that they should check the box where they get to keep the things the seller leaves behind. That way they don't have to worry about throwing anything away that they don't want).

Form 22J Any property built before 1977 has to include a disclosure related to lead based paint.

Form 22K -Lists utility companies that service the property?

Form 35 Inspection contingency. If you have an inspection contingency then this would say how many days you have to inspect the property, how many days the seller has to decide if they are going to fix anything, and how long they have to fix it if they agree to it.

Form 35E this is the escalation clause. If you choose to use this form then you would fill in the blanks that say you are willing to pay a certain amount MORE than the next highest offer up to the amount that you choose.

These are just some of the most used forms, there are many many more depending on how you want to make your offer and depending on the property (if it has septic, etc).

6

My Offer is Accepted Now What?.

Your earnest money check will be cashed.

If you have an inspection contingency then you need to hire an inspector. If you are making an offer without an inspection contingency then you should have already inspected the property. You should be present for the inspection. It can easily take 3 hours or more. The inspector will get into the crawl space, up in the attic, check the wiring and appliances. By the time she is done, a good inspector will even be able to tell you which door knobs are loose!

If you have a normal inspection contingency then you will have a certain number of days in which to inform the seller whether or not you want to buy the property. This number would have been one that you agreed to on the Form 35. During this time you can walk away without even having a. If you do not respond to the seller within this time then it is the same as approving the inspection. You might decide to ask the seller to fix some things that are wrong (there are always things wrong with any house).

If you get past the inspection then it is time to apply for the loan. It is possible to apply for the loan before the inspection is done but many people choose to wait. You would have a certain number of days from mutual acceptance to apply for the loan. This time frame would be on the 22A Finance Addendum. After you apply for the loan then the loan officer will schedule the appraisal.

The appraisal will take about 10-15 days. If it comes in below the purchase price then you usually don't have to buy it (if you have a normal finance contingency.

If the appraisal is low then usually the seller agrees to lower the price part way and the buyer agrees to add to the down payment. This is unless you have agreed to waive all or part of the appraisal as part of your offer. In order to make your offer more competitive you may have agreed to pay extra to cover all or part of the difference between the low appraisal and the price.

If you have made it past the appraisal then you are now ready to for closing! This may only take a couple more weeks. It takes time for the lender to create all the documents they want you to sign.

The Escrow Company might schedule the seller to sign at this time. It is possible that the seller could sign all their documents a week or more before closing.

The lender will put together disclosures which you are REQUIRED to have at least 3 days before closing. No one not even the buyer can shorten this time frame. When you get this is probably when escrow will schedule a day for you to sign.

It is surprising but the actual documents that the lender wants you to sign may not be available until the very last day that you are required to purchase the property. It can easily be over a 100 pages.

You go to the escrow company office to sign the documents. They can also send someone to your house with the documents for you to sign at your convenience.

The next day the escrow company gives the documentation to a courier who gets it to the court house by the end of the day at which point the sale is recorded with the county...and you bought a house!

7

I'm a Seller
What advice do I get?

Go back and read the first chapter where I give advice to buyers on how to compete. This will give context to the rest of this chapter.

It is a seller's market. If you play your cards right then you can get multiple offers with escalation clauses and no inspection contingencies. The escalation clause is a one page form that says that the buyer will pay X amount more than the next highest offer up to a limit they choose. If you get the buyers excited enough then they will pick a very high limit (one that they hope they don't have to pay).

In order to get the most offers as possible I like to remove barriers to entry. Buyers know that they need to pre-inspect the property before making an offer so that they can waive that contingency. This costs around $600. You can imagine how expensive this might be for buyers after they lost 3 bidwars. They may not go after your property because they are only partly interested and they don't want to risk another $600. If you remove this barrier then you increase the number of escalation clauses which likely increases the highest price.

I always encourage sellers to hire an inspector then provide the report to prospective buyers for free. Yes you may find something wrong that you have to disclose...but the buyer will find it anyway when they do their own inspection. If you don't do it this way -and the buyer finds a major problem- then they are likely to inflate the nature of the problem as a negotiation ploy, at which point you would be wise to hire your own expert to look at the problem anyway. Best to get in front of a problem -even one you don't know you have.

The median market time in Seattle is 7 days. I am surprised how many sellers I run into who know that the word median means "half" who also believe that ALL homes are selling in 7 days or less!

If a home is on the market for more than 7 days then the new median market time is around 30 days. This means that a house on the market for more than 7 days has a 50% chance of still being for sale 30 days later.

A popular strategy right now is to list a property on Wednesday or Thursday and then put a bid review date of the following Tuesday or Wednesday. If you want to use this strategy then you need to be really certain that the property is priced right.

Buyers usually assume that the property will sell for 10% more than the list price. They may think it is worth the list price but if they don't think it is worth MORE than the list price then they might not make an offer on the bid review date.

If the bid review date comes and goes without an offer then you will find it very difficult to get the listing price at that point. This is because buyers will assume that there is something wrong with the property. Buyers usually won't even look at listings online if they are more than 10 days old. They won't even go back to see if it is still for sale! I have seen this many times.

What if the bid review date comes along and you have no offers? Sometimes lowering the price by 5% or more is the best strategy. In the Northwest Multiple Listing Service a price change of 5% or more will cause it to pop up as a new listing online (even on 3rd party websites!) I actually RAISED the price by 5% on a listing and sold it in 10 days even though it was previously listed by another company for over 200 days (and it sold for more than the previous list price).

You can increase the chances of multiple offers by getting as many people as possible to view the property and by removing barriers to entry for people who might want to make an offer.

You need to find ways to pack the open houses with as many people as possible. My theory is that you need at least 2 buyers to write offers with escalation clauses (more is way better) If only two buyers are interested then you want them to be surrounded by people at the open houses (even if everyone else is a looky-loo). This will increase their anxiety and hopefully cause them to be aggressive on their escalation clause.

Most brokers don't bother sending out post cards to advertise an open house. Some send out a few. I like to send out 500 -not because I think one of them will actually buy the house but because I want the open houses to be packed!

Photos are very important. Remember you want as many people to come look at the property as soon as possible after it is listed -if for no other reason than to get serious buyers excited about competition. I am SHOCKED at how many sellers let the listing broker get a way with terrible mobile phone photos. Your broker is making thousands and thousands of dollars..make them pay for stuff. Terrible photos tell buyers that you aren't a serious seller....besides your listing broker should be paying for these anyway! I typically spend around $300 for professional photos. She comes in with multiple remote control flash bulbs on tripods. It is a professional operation that takes about an hour.

Staging is critical. I have heard estimates that staging will increase the price of a home by 7-10%....staging usually costs around $3,000. Do the math. I like to use minimal staging. In a small bedroom I might put a queen size bed and a night stand. Just enough furniture so buyers can see that their stuff will fit. There are different and valid other staging strategies but successful brokers know that staging is critical. Whether or not your broker pays for it is negotiable.

What happens if you get multiple offers? Well lets say the price is $700k and you have 5 offers. You might have 2 around the list price, a cash offer that escalates to a limit of $720k, a financed offer with a small earnest money deposit that escalates to $770k in $5k incriments, and a financed offer that escalates to $755k in $2k increments with a large earnest money deposit. Of course they should have all pre-inspected the property. You can pretty much throw away any offer that has an inspection contingency when you have several that don't. That is because the inspection contingency is a "walk away" clause.

Your highest offer is really $760k from the person with the low earnest money deposit. This is because they escalated by $5k increments which puts them $5k over the offer with high earnest money. You can pick any offer you want and you might find that the offer for $755k with a high earnest money is better than the one for $760k. You might even go back to the cash offer and see if they will come up to $760k. They might say that they will come up to $740k but they will close in two weeks.

I prepare my sellers that it could take 4, 5, or 6 hours to get through the back and forth. It can take a buyer an hour or more to answer a question because they need to talk to their partner, check their bank account, call their lender, etc. multiply that times multiple offers. Many times I worked until midnight on a day when the offer deadline was 5pm! It is a rough way to spend an evening no matter which side you are on.

8

Real Transactions

Central Area Craftsman

I had a listing on a beautiful example of a craftsman house in early January. It was listed for $650,000. We had a total of 7 offers. 3 of the offers were around $750,000. I went to the top 3 bidders and found one who would waive $50,000 of the appraisal. The property appraised at $700,000, so the buyer had to pay an additional
$50,000 on top of the downpayment. The funny (not so funny) thing about this is that 3 weeks later, there were 2 more similar craftsmans for sale in the same neighborhood.

Basically, we would have been lucky to get $650,000 had the other 2 homes been on the market at the same time. Instead, my listing became a comparable sale when it came time to appraise the other 2 houses!

January Condo

Prices had been going up from Fall to January around 10–15%. Sometimes more for lower priced real estate. I was asked to provide a price opinion and list a small one bedroom condo in January.

Only 2 years earlier they had been selling for around $200,000 but there were some sales from the previous Fall for around $275,000. So I decided that we should list it for $300,000. I like to use round numbers because they tend to be natural starting and stopping points for people when they are entering their criteria into their favorite real estate search site. If it sold for the list price then it would be the highest price for a one bedroom unit in the history of the project (it was by no means the best one) I felt it was achievable but I wasn't so confident as to put a bid review date on the listing. Instead I told brokers that the seller would review offers upon receipt. Well this really freaked out people because they felt they had to look at it right now since they didn't have until next Tuesday to make an offer. My phone was ringing off the hook and by the very next day I had several people interested in writing offers.

We had three offers in three days. They were $320,000, $325,000 and $330,000. All of the offers had finance contingencies. I didn't think the appraisal was going to justify the price, so I told the buyers to waive the appraisal. I had one buyer who offered to waive up to $10k of the appraisal. This was the $320k offer. The seller could accept the $330,000 offer but if the condo only appraised at $300,000 then that is all the seller would get. I convinced the seller to accept the $320,000 offer because I didn't think that the condo was going to appraise much over the list price. It appraised at $300k, meaning that the buyer was going to have to pay $310, requiring the buyer to bring an additional $10k to add to their down payment. The seller made $10,000 more by taking an offer $10,000 less than the highest one.

Now, the funny thing about all of this is that the seller was mad at ME! He felt that I didn't earn my commission because I sold it in only 3 days! He said he could have sold it himself. I asked him if he would have known to ask for the buyer to waive the appraisal. He said "no". I said, "... so I made you $10k more than if you didn't list it!" It took him a couple of days to swallow, but he ultimately understood that it isn't about the amount of time spent working on this problem; it is that I knew where to tap the pipe with my wrench.

Auburn House

The property had been listed for about 200 days by a discount broker. The original list price was $640k, but they had lowered the price several times so that it was currently $575k. The owner contacted me because they work with someone I had done two successful transactions with. The house was 3,700 sqft and particularly large for the neighborhood—3700sqft in an area where very few are larger than 2900 sqft. I did some research and discovered that a large subdivision nearby had sold approximately two dozen brand new houses larger than 3000sqft over the previous 9 months at
a price of $620–$670k. The seller and the listing broker did not apparently realise that they had been competing with brand new homes over the previous 9 months. I also learned that there were only 3 more left, and there wouldn't be any more for approximately 6 months. So now was the opportunity. When the listing with the other agency expired, they listed it with me. I RAISED the price to $605k, and we didn't do a thing to the house to justify a price increase. We sold it in 10 days for $585k after it had been on the market with another agency for 200 days for $575k! I knew that if we made a 5% price change, then it would show up as a new listing in the MLS. The vast majority of buyers will not go back to see if an old listing is still on the market because they would think that something is wrong with it, but this strategy allowed us to be viewed by buyers that had just recently entered the market.

Receiver House

A house—which had been taken over by the city to satisfy a judgement—was for sale. The property was the responsibility of a receiver. A receiver is a person that the city put in charge to make all decisions about the property. The house was in such disrepair that that it made more sense to build something new rather than fix it. My clients thought they could put 3 townhomes on it, even though by all appearances the site could only handle 2 townhomes. Knowing there were going to be many competing offers, they asked me how much they should offer. I suggested that we use an escalator clause that tops out at $25k more than a very aggressive bidder would pay for a 2-home development site. This buyer would have paid $100,000 more but no one wants to pay more than they have to.

Late in the morning of the day when bids were due, we were told that our offer was the highest at the time. Our offer was $425k. After a few hours had passed with no additional information, I called the listing broker and learned that 2 other higher offers came in and that they had made a counter offer to the people in the first position. I asked what the counter offer was, wouldn't tell me but he explained that he asked the other buyer to cross out a section which removes the buyer's ability to back out in case of misstatements by the seller. Well, this is actually common practice in this hot market, and we had already crossed it out on our offer. I had reason to believe that the 1st highest offer was from an overseas investor. My experience was such that overseas investors do not like to cross out that section; they perceive it as suspicious should they be asked to cross this section out...frankly I don't blame them.

After 2 hours went by with no word, I suggested to my buyer that I didn't think the first place offer was going to cross out that section and that we should totally re-write the first page of our offer with a higher price—$450k. I felt it was important to re-write the offer with the new price rather than crossing it out and initialing the change. Receivers, in particular, like to have things very 'clean.' Well, another hour passed, and we learned that the receiver took our offer! It turned out that the first place offer refused to cross out the section, so the receiver told the listing broker to get a 'best and final' bid from the next two highest offers. The listing broker said that he already had one (from us), so the receiver said, "Great! We will accept that one!" It was the first offer I wrote for this client, and we won against thirty other offers! A year later, they sold the property for 70% more than they paid for it.

Low Down Payment Buyer
In Seattle, the median market time is 7 days, and everything is a bid war. This was just starting to be the case in the suburb of Kirkland a couple of years ago. The median market time had just dropped to around a week, but not every listing agent was implementing a bid deadline. The next best thing to cash in a bid war is an offer with no inspection and a large down payment. For some reason, sellers value a buyer with a high down payment possibly because they believe that the buyer will be able to withstand an unforeseen circumstance and still close the deal. In this case, I had a first-time home buyer with 5% down. The thing about this part of Kirkland is that several square miles of this neighborhood was built at the same time in the 70s, so it made it very easy to 'comp.'

My buyer found a house they really loved. The price was $440k. There was no bid date set up. The seller was willing to look at offers as she received them.

We visited the property on day 2, after which period I called the listing broker to see if he was going to do a bid date. Sometimes the listing broker will decide to implement a bid review date after the initial listing. I also commiserated with him about what a shame it is that low down payment buyers are having such a hard time. He agreed.

I then called about 6 similar properties that were pending (the market was moving so fast that pending comps would likely be higher than sold comps). Pending is different than Pending Inspection. Pending means that the inspection has been completed or is waived.

I learned that comparable properties were going for around 5% more than the list price. So I explained this to the listing broker and asked him how he would feel if we wrote an offer 5% over list the list price with a 1-day inspection. I explained that this would be doing his seller a favor, which he agreed. And then it appraised $5k MORE than we offered!

A bid war situation is VERY stressful for the seller. You would think it would be a happy time, but what actually happens is that you may have 10 offers all with escalation clauses, but they are different enough to cause distress. For example, the highest offers typically have the sketchiest financing, while the lowest offers tend to be all-cash with no financing. Then you might go back to the highest offer and talk to their lender. If the price is so high that it might not appraise at that value, they will partially waive the appraisal, or they might say no. So, then, you go to your next favorite offer and see if they will do better, and they say they have to talk to their partner, and they get back to you in about an hour with a slightly different proposal which maybe makes you want to talk to one of the cash offers to see if they want to pay more. This can definitely go on for 5 hours. That is why I never have offers come in after noon—because it is stressful for everyone to be putting the final touches on a contract negotiation after 11 p.m. at night!

Contingent Sale

A contingent sale is a sale that is contingent on the buyer's other house selling first. In fact I did recently do one. The house to be sold wasn't even listed yet!

This happened less than 2 years ago. We will call the seller M. She had been getting her house ready for market while she was also looking for a condo to buy in Seattle. We were about 2 weeks away from listing her house when we found the perfect condo with a 180 degree view of Lake Union! The condo had just blown past its bid review date with no offers. It is fairly common for houses to get NO offers on the bid review date (in spite of what you hear in the news).

The seller and listing broker of the condo had put it on the market without staging or even bothering to clean or paint it. After they had no offers on it, they decided to go back to square one and do everything right. By then it was too late because it had been on the market for about 15 days.

Buyers in this market think there is something wrong with a property if it has been on the market more than about 10 days (usually its true). I realized that it was actually a good price and that the listing broker had simply mis-marketed the unit. The best strategy for the seller when this happens is to drop the price 5% right away and hope to get a bid war started at the lower price. A 5% price drop will make the listing show up as a new listing the MLS and other websites.

I told the listing broker that I would bring him a full price offer but it had to be contingent on the sale of M's house in Kirkland that was going to be listed the following week. My buyer wanted to come in with a lower price but I am a believer of the old adage that you can have your price or your terms but rarely both. They both agreed -M sold her house and bought the condo which appraised $15,000 more than she paid for it!

There are a lot of lessons in this story but I can't stress enough that most real estate agents are better at getting your business than they are at doing their job. Luckily in this case I managed to save the listing broker and the seller from having to lower the price while also getting a great deal for my buyer.

For Sale by Owner Nightmare

I was acquainted with a couple that had separated. They had missed some payments on their house and were probably going to be foreclosed on within a few months. They wanted to sell their house but they didn't want to pay a real estate agent so they offered it For Sale by Owner. I didn't even know they were selling their house.

A real estate agent came along and offered to sell it for NO commission to a developer and that he would represent the buyer (the developer). The agent disclosed that he was a partner of the developer which is why he was doing it for no commission. They gave the seller $450,000.

This gave the couple $10,000 to split after paying off the loan and back payments. The exwife and 2 kids were now looking for low income rental housing.

The developers remodeled the house for $150,000 and built a new house in the back yard. Both houses sold for $750,000. This means that the developer paid $0.00! for the lot to build on....a value of $175,000 plus made $100,000 on the remodel of the existing house, plus their profit on the new house. I later ran into the developer and asked him if he would have paid $175k more and he said "absolutely".

So the exwife got $5,000 and had to find low income housing instead of her share of $185,000. Even if they had paid a full commission to have a full service realtor represent them and list it on the MLS they still would have made around $150,000 to split.

Retirement House

John had lived in the Central Area of Seattle for over 30 years and probably didn't repair his house even one time. I think he paid about $20,000 for his house. He was a gruff old guy who always wore stained t-shirts. His idea of getting his house ready for showing was to put his bong in the sink. A lot of people thought he was a tough old man and no rocket scientist but I learned to appreciate his sense of humor and his company. John wasn't particularly on the corporate fast track and at the age of 64 I think he was making around $12 an hour as a local delivery driver. One amazing thing that he did was to make all of his house payments and never refinance. His house was free and clear. We sold his beat-up old house for around $350,000 and found him a totally remodeled rambler in Burien for $250,000. This was his retirement, modest as it may be. He now had a beautiful new house that he owed no money on and $100.000 in the bank to supplement his fixed income retirement income. I have known many people whose retirement mainly consisted of a house that they never refinanced. Markets may go up and down but one thing for sure is that if you keep making your payments then you will gain equity in your house. After around 6 or 7 years half of your payment goes towards paying down the loan.

9

Common Questions

But how can I compete against an all cash offer?
Only a few things separate a cash offer from a financed offer. A cash offer usually closes in about 2 weeks. They typically can't close any faster due to the amount of time needed by the Escrow and Title Companies. A cash offer is not subject to a financing contingency. There is no appraisal. Cash offers however also tend to be at the lower end of the price range. This is why, if you have a financed offer at a higher price, pre-underwriting by your lender is so important. It allows you to close faster and it gives the seller confidence that the loan will be successful. You can also simply waive the finance contingency. This puts your offer on almost the same footing as cash however you will lose you earnest money if you aren't not able to close.

Close with cash from a commercial loan
This is not for owner occupied property. If you are an investor you might consider getting a commercial loan to buy the property and then cashing it out with conventional financing after closing. They typically don't do an appraisal and can give you approval within a day or two. You will wind up paying a few percentage points of the loan amount but this can be a good deal if your seller is willing to discount the price for the security

of a real cash offer. These types of loans can usually close within 2 weeks.

How much does a buyer's broker cost?

Usually NOTHING for the buyer. That's right. If you are a buyer, your broker will likely cost you nothing at all, but they are still required by the State of Washington to look after your interests and not the seller's. Both brokers are typically compensated by the seller. The listing broker has already negotiated the amount of commission with the seller. The listing broker then shares his commission with the buyer's broker at a predetermined amount. Listing brokers do not expect to represent both sides of the transaction; it happens less than 1% of the time. Many listing brokers, in fact, do not want the liability of having responsibilities to both the seller and the buyer.

What is the Multiple Listing Service (MLS)?

This is an organization to which almost every residential real estate agent belongs. All MLS members have to also be a Realtor. Think of it as a private website where data of all listings by members are required to be uploaded. This website is where Zillow-type websites obtain their information. Websites like Zillow will download raw data from the MLS every 15 minutes or more. These websites only display some of the information; in fact, they can't download all of it. Only a broker who is a member of the MLS can see all the data. A member of the MLS can see all the listing data on every listed property, including private brokers' remarks. Additionally, members of the MLS have all agreed to use the same forms. All brokers of an MLS will use the same forms for the purchase and sale agreement; some individual brokerage companies may have additional attachments.

How does Zillow work?

Brokers buy advertising in different zip codes from Zillow. When you visit Zillow in a zip code for which I bought advertising, then you will see my name next to the property. Zillow features three agents next to whatever properties you happen to be looking at. Typically, this is not the listing broker, which is fine because the listing broker works for the seller anyway. This is a great way to meet agents who are successful enough to afford their advertising. Many people believe that the different agents listed next to a property on Zillow work together. The chances are that we don't know each other.

Who is a Realtor?

According to the National Association of Realtors, a REALTOR® is a licensed real estate salesperson who belongs to the National Association of REALTORS®, the largest trade group in the country. Every agent is not a REALTOR®, but most are. If you're unsure, you can ask your agent if they're a licensed REALTOR®. REALTORS® are held to a higher ethical standard than licensed agents and must adhere to a Code of Ethics.

Who is an Agent vs. a Broker?

This varies by state. In the State of Washington, all real estate agents are called Brokers. A Managing Broker is a Broker that has had significant additional education and has passed exams so as to be certified by the State to be qualified to run a brokerage office.

What is a team?

You might see signs for the ABC Team of XYC Real Estate Company. A team leader may be someone with many years of experience (and frequently not) who then hires newbies to follow up on leads they have purchased. Team members typically give up a percentage of their commissions to the team leader. I recently heard a stat that the average team member only stays with the team for around 18 months. This is because they start to wonder why they are giving up a percentage of their income. Often the team leader is more interested in being a boss than actually selling real estate. The team leader also gets to take some credit for all their team members' sales, which can make their statistics inflated. The chances are that your basic team member has not been in the business very long at all.

What is Escrow?

An Escrow Company is a neutral third party that facilitates the transaction. You give them the down payment and earnest money. Your broker hands them the purchase and sale agreement. Your lender sends the escrow your loan documents. The escrow schedules a time for you to sign the loan documents. The Escrow Company also schedules a time for the seller to come in and sign the documents transferring the property to you. Your bank sends in the money that you borrowed and hands it to the seller and then hands you the papers to the property.

What is Earnest Money?

Earnest Money is a good faith deposit that is held in an escrow and is refundable to you for a few specific reasons ... called contingencies.

What are Contingencies?

In a normal market, you might have an inspection contingency. This is a period of time, usually a few days, during which you can inspect the property, and you can usually back out of the transaction and have your earnest money refunded to you for any reason at all. This type of contingency is sometimes called a Walk-Away clause because you can back out for no reason.

Obviously, sellers don't like this so much, but in a normal market, it is typical. In a hot market, it is only the offers with no inspection contingency that will be considered. Buyers in this case would typically pay to have an independent inspector inspect the property prior to making an offer (this is usually a 3-hour process which can cost as much as $500 or more).

The other contingency is a finance contingency, which usually allows you to back out and get your earnest money refunded if you lose your financing during a set period of time before closing— through NO FAULT OF YOUR OWN. You can't just go torpedo your own financing.

What is Title Insurance?
According to The State of Washington Insurance Commissioner, what Title Insurance does for you is, when you buy real estate, you're buying all the assets and liabilities associated with that property. It proves the seller has legal authority to sell the property. Ensures there are no liens. Covers problems due to fraud, legal issues and divorce claims in transferring title. Protects you from prior forgeries, mistakes in legal documents and inheritance. Protects you against someone challenging your ownership of the property.

Who needs to buy Title Insurance?
You'll need it if you buy real estate in Washington state and you use a mortgage lender to finance it. You'll need to have both lender and home owner insurance :

Lender Title Insurance:
Your lender will require you to buy a lender title insurance policy equal to the amount of your loan. It protects your lender up to the amount of their loan, but it doesn't protect your

interest in the property. Even if you refinance, you'll need to buy lender title insurance. It will protect the lender from any issues that have come up since you bought the property, such as liens or easements.

Owner Title Insurance:
To protect your interest, you'll need an owner's title policy for the full price you paid for the property. Generally, most sellers pay for the owner's policy.

What is The Purchase and Sale Agreement?
Your offer will be made by filling out the blanks on a collection of forms that the MLS has provided to your broker. Your broker will ask you questions that will help them fill it out for you, e.g., "How much Earnest Money do you feel comfortable with?" "What type of financing are you using?" And of course the price. The typical purchase and sale agreement has around 22 pages. The inspection contingency, finance contingency, earnest money are all included in this document.

What is an Escalation Clause?
In a competitive environment, a typical winning offer will have an Escalation Clause attached to it. This is a one-page form that simply says that you will pay X amount more than the next higher offer up to an amount that you choose. So, for a $600,000 house, it might say I will pay $5,000 more than the next highest offer up to $660,000.

What is the Form 17 Seller Disclosure
In the State of Washington all sellers must provide a list of disclosures to potential buyer...even if it is a private sale that does not involve a real estate agent. The MLS has a special form

which serves that purpose called the Form 17. Usually the listing broker will have this available when the property is listed.

The buyer has 3 days to back out of the transaction from when they receive the Form 17. A buyer making a competitive offer will sign the lines where they acknowledge receipt of the Form 17 and also waiving the 3 day review period.

If the seller doesn't give you the Form 17 until the day before closing.....then you still have 3 days to decide if you want to buy the property.

What is a Condominium Resale Certificate

If the property is a condominium, then you would also get a Resale Certificate which is a list of disclosures made by the condominium association. The attachments to this form could be hundreds of pages long! It may include a Reserve Study which is a report completed by a 3rd party that analyzies all the systems and aspects of the condominium complex and estimates the expected life span of each of those items. It also analyzises whether or not the association is collecting enough dues to pay for those items when they are ready to be replaced. The report might say that the roof will last another 8-12 years and then indicate the cost of replacement and whether or not the association is collecting enough money.

What's a banker and a mortgage broker?

Bankers are typically loaning you the money that they have whereas a mortgage broker might submit your application to a variety of other lenders which could be banks or a different types of wall street investors. Sometimes mortgage brokers can find an investor with more flexible criteria but sometimes it is best to go where they know you already.

Can I get down payment assistance?

The Washington State Housing Finance Commission has a variety of programs where they can loan you part of the down payment. You might be able to buy a house with as little as 1% down if you and the house meets all the qualifications. Contact me for details.

Home Advantage also offers downpayment assistance. This second mortgage loan program has a 0% interest rate, payment deferred for 30 years, and combines with the Home Advantage first mortgage loan program. Borrowers must meet the income limits for the Home Advantage Program first mortgage.

To be eligible for a Home Advantage downpayment assistance loan, you must not exceed the following income limits: Statewide $97,000

Borrowers must attend a Commission-sponsored homebuyer seminar prior to reserving funds under the Home Advantage Program. Cash back to borrowers is not allowed.

Eligible households in all counties may qualify for a maximum loan amount of up to 4.00% of the total loan amount or up to 5% using our conventional HFA Preferred loan.

A participating loan officer can help you determine the sales price you can afford, how much cash you will need to close, and how much you can borrow on a Home Advantage loan.

Home Advantage also offers Needs Based Downpayment Assistance. This second mortgage loan program has a 1% interest rate, payment deferred for 30 years, and also combines with the Home Advantage first mortgage loan program.

Please inquire with your lender to see if you qualify for a loan amount of up to $10,000.

Maximum loan limit as of 04/13/20188
To be eligible for a Home Advantage Downpayment Assistance Needs Based loan, you must not exceed the following income limits:

King/Snohomish $97,000

All Other Counties $81,100

Veterans
There is no assessment of need for Veterans to be eligible for the $10,000 loan amount.

Home buyer education
Borrowers must attend a Commission-sponsored homebuyer seminar prior to reserving funds under the Home Advantage Program. Cash back to borrowers is not allowed.

I am a certified instructor for the required class. Let me know if you would like me to schedule one for you (its free) or if you would like me to put you in touch with a qualified lender.

I appreciate you taking the time to read my book. Please contact me with any suggestions, questions, or comments.

Dan Sanchez
Managing Broker for Coldwell Banker Danforth

Home Buyer Instructor for the Washington State Housing
Finance Commission.

I have over 20 years' experience in both commercial and residential real estate brokerage. I started my career in the late 1980s finding land for custom home builders. I went on to work for the Chairman of one of the largest property management companies in America. I spent 8 years acquiring and brokering large apartment complexes nationwide for Pension Funds, Insurance Companies, and private investors. During this time I was appointed by a bankruptcy court judge to be treasurer of a 300 unit condominium project. I remodeled dozens of homes and designed 2 subdivisions.

In 1999 I wrote a 20,000-line application in ASP which was used by institutional investors to analyze investment properties. It tracked over 1,000,000 units of apartments throughout the nation.

All of my businesses failed almost immediately after the start of the post 9/11 economy. This was a devastating loss that took many years to recover from. After much soul searching and lesson learning, I have come to realize that helping actual people not corporations is what I find truly rewarding. The best days are when I give a new buyer their new keys.

My clients include International Executives, First Time Home Buyers, and Investors. I am a Managing Broker and am a certified instructor for the Washington Housing Finance Commission. I was recently Chair of the Central Area Neighborhood District Council and currently sit on a variety of community boards and councils in Seattle.

Made in the USA
San Bernardino, CA
03 July 2018